SURVIVAL
SECRETS
OF
MIDDLE
SCHOOL

by

Ross Cooper
Jelani Brooks
Alexandra Clark
Anthony Eaton, Jr.
Brandon Joyner
Kayla Joyner
Lauren Joyner
Brianna Latham
Jeffrey Lewis
Cameron Lucas
Jay Pendarvis, Jr.
Gabrielle Stevenson
Aria Townes
Malachi Walker
Christopher Wong

Printed by CreateSpace, an Amazon.com Company

DEDICATION

To Middle Schoolers ~ Past, Present and Future

ACKNOWLEDGMENTS

The Teen Foundation Committee of the Alexandria-Mount Vernon Chapter of Jack and Jill of America, Inc. would like to thank the following persons for their assistance in the production of this book:

Mrs. Suzanne Walker
Mrs. Sandra Jenkins Clark
Dr. Debra Henry
Mrs. Keisha Brooks
Dr. Tiffany Latham
Mrs. Lia Pendarvis
Mrs. Keri McCoy, Esq.
Mr. Thomas Henry
Ms. Candice Taylor

FOREWORD

Changes, challenges and choices mark the middle school years. Members of the Teen Group of the Alexandria-Mount Vernon Chapter of Jack and Jill of America, Inc. have authored *Survival Secrets of Middle School*, an anthology of essays, based on their own experiences. In this way, they hope to help other young people who are currently in this phase of life. The topics covered are as diverse as the adolescents who wrote them. From managing lockers to bullying to approaching teachers, each chapter has at least one "secret" that has helped the individual writer persevere.

As the adults who have supervised this endeavor, we are proud of the Teen Group's efforts to compose, publish and promote this book. It was written not only to aid individual tweens and teens but also to raise money to support charitable work. The contributors will not earn money from this project; rather, all royalties from the book will be donated to the Jack and Jill of America Foundation. This organization assists other organizations in creating opportunities for children to build character and learn leadership skills.

Whether you are a middle schooler, parent, teacher or administrator, we trust that you will be enlightened by *Survival Secrets of Middle School*. We also hope that all who read this book will survive and thrive!

~Suzanne Walker, Chapter President
~Sandra Clark, Chapter Teen Advisor
~Debra Henry, Chapter Teen Foundation Committee Advisor

CONTENTS

INTRODUCTION

The idea for this book was conceived by the Teens of the Alexandria-Mount Vernon Chapter of Jack and Jill of America, Inc. as a way to raise funds for the Jack and Jill Foundation. Many meetings and conference calls took place to execute the countless decisions to produce this book. For the Teen Foundation Committee, this was a labor of love on behalf of all middle schoolers. As the committee chair, co-author and teen editor-in-chief, I hope this will help middle schoolers to better understand how one can best persevere during this time of life. It is a learning experience!

~Ross Cooper
Teen Foundation Chair

SURVIVAL
SECRETS
OF
MIDDLE
SCHOOL

SURVIVAL SECRET:
Never give anyone your locker combination.

CHAPTER 1
Lockers

Don't worry about going to middle school. You'll be fine. One of the first of many experiences of a new middle school student is the assignment of a locker.

The locker is the place for your books and papers so that you don't have to carry them around all day. You'll be going from class to class instead of staying in one room as you did in elementary school.

Your locker is not to be feared. You can stow pencils, extra supplies and your jacket. All you really have to worry about with the locker is to remember where it is located and what is the combination.

Don't let your mother buy a lot of locker décor like mirrors, shelves, stickers, trash cans, wet wipes, toiletry items and unnecessary stuff. You will not be cool if you have all of those items. In fact, a messy locker is very cool because no one can make you clean it. You have to be organized only to the point that you can find the homework papers or books that you need.

Lockers can be a good place for socializing. You can get to know the people with lockers in close proximity to yours. But remember: Never give anyone your locker combination; he or she may put his or her trash in your locker. Especially, don't give your combination to a girlfriend; middle school relationships have a very short attention span. You may get sabotaged by a scorned ex.

Don't put food in your locker. It will smell and it could encourage creepy crawly things to find their way into your locker.

Don't try to get inside your locker. The new modern lockers are probably too small anyway, but if you have ever watched old TV shows where kids hide in lockers, you will soon learn that trying it is not a good idea. Also, don't try to put any other kid in your locker. You will get in trouble.

Your locker is not your bedroom. Don't bring expensive electronics, games or music and leave them in your locker. Believe it or not, lockers can be broken into.

Don't ever put anything in your locker that could get you in trouble if school officials found out. They have the combination to all the lockers in the school. This is necessary because you might forget your combination and you may have to ask them for it again.

Except for science and physical education, classes where you are not allowed to have a backpack, the locker is not even necessary. If you are running late, you may not have time to stop there between classes to get things out of it. You can carry your things in the backpack and never even use your locker. An empty locker makes end of school year a breeze.

Good luck in middle school. Study hard and get good grades. You'll be glad you did!

Malachi Walker
~12th grade

SURVIVAL SECRET:
Decisions made are hard when done
under peer pressure.

CHAPTER 2
Judgment

So, the new kid at school comes up to talk to you and you immediately think that she is not cool just by the way she dresses and speaks. Instead of being polite, you are really rude. Next thing you know, your friends are talking to the new kid and aren't hanging out with you. The lessons from this experience are: always make a good first impression and never judge a book by its cover. You should always use good judgment or the consequences could be very unfortunate.

Judgment in relationships is a common form of evaluation used by middle schoolers. This is used especially to help people decide whom to hang with or whom to work with inside and outside of school. When using this form of judgment to decide with whom to hang out, be sure that you know the individual or individuals very well. Even if you think that you know a person really well, you never know exactly what that individual will do in public.

Good relationship with teachers also requires judgment decisions that not only will help you in class but also will help you in the future. If you ever have to get a letter of recommendation for a program or for a college application, it is beneficial to have decent relationships with your teachers. This advice also applies to relationships with staff, administrators, counselors and noncore subject teachers.

While you may think that relationship judgment is the only form of judgment you'll use in middle school, there's another that's even more prevalent: peer pressure judgment. Decisions made while under peer pressure can be hard. You will make difficult choices between right and what will probably turn out to be wrong. These types of decisions occur when trying to find a friend with whom to hang out. Please know that the popular crowd may not be the right crowd for you. Peer pressure can also be exerted when making decisions about going to places such as the mall or sneaking into the movies. If you're in similar situations, it is extremely important that you look out for your own interest and decide which choice will be best for you.

Trust also should play a huge role in your decisions. You may think: "My friends always look out for me. Anything they do must be OK; so why not try it." But this is the wrong mind-set with which to approach such situations. Quick decisions like this could damage your life permanently. So when making such choices, you should look at the possible outcome of each alternative decision. This is also known as a "pros and cons" list.

You don't necessarily have to write the list down literally. Sometimes, you just do it mentally. Once you've evaluated each of your options, that's when you make the best choice. This process can also be used for various scenarios such as what to do with friends on the weekend or in deciding whether or not you should skip a class.

There's one more form of judgment. It relates to curriculum choices. This is something you face in middle school that can force you to make some difficult choices. Curriculum judgment can be hard to handle at times especially when your decisions will separate you from your friends and prevent you from talking during the school day. When choosing your courses each year, make sure to choose classes that will benefit you. If you pick a class that everyone chooses, make sure that you're not going to that class just because you don't want to be by yourself or away from your friends. Also, don't choose a class that's too challenging in order to brag about it to your friends and to make them think that you're smarter than they are. In fact, you would be doing yourself more harm than good.

Judgment has to be used correctly or the consequences could be very unfortunate. To prevent yourself from using it incorrectly, please take into consideration the ideas that I have suggested and use them to the best of your ability. These include being careful to observe people's actions to determine if you should hang out with them, work with them or even associate with them at all. Also, maintain good relationships with your teachers and other school officials. In conclusion, be mindful of what you say and how you judge because middle school will be the first of many places where you'll make tough decisions.

Brianna Latham
~8th grade

SURVIVAL SECRET:
Cherish your body type.

CHAPTER 3
Body Image

Everybody wants other people to think that they are attractive, but sometimes our definition of attractiveness can become distorted. Everyone's body type is different and you shouldn't aspire to look just like a certain person or a certain body type. In middle school, your body is in the stage of puberty and you are still growing; most likely you will not be finished growing until you are in college. Girls are constantly put under immense pressure to have all of the right looks. Not all girls are able to achieve the "ideal" body and some that do may have had the help of a plastic surgeon. Your genes determine what your body will look like. Of course, diet and exercise play an important role. Your area of focus shouldn't be on looking like a professional model, but on maintaining your own body type. Having a large butt, chest or thigh gap doesn't make you superior or inferior to someone who does not have such features. Personally, I wish that I was born with dimples in my cheeks, but life doesn't always work out the way you want. I've learned to make the most of the natural beauty with which I was born and to focus on the parts that I like instead of the parts that I dislike.

For boys, there is constant pressure to have bulging muscles and a defined jaw line. Again, these features are considered to be ideal or beautiful in mainstream media. It takes regular exercise and diet to maintain large muscles, so your muscles shouldn't pop out of your shirt. If you try to work out, use caution because overworking your body can lead to future injuries. As previously stated, middle schoolers are still growing.

The human body is very complicated inside and outside. There are many different body shapes and not everyone falls under one particular type. Female body shapes can range from apple, pear and hourglass to spoon, oval and diamond. Male body types are generally ectomorphic or slender body build, endomorphic or fat type of body build, or mesomorphic, the athletic physical body type. You should take the time to research your own specific body type and shape and shop for your clothes according to your shape. Just remember that since you are still in your early teens, your body might lean towards one shape now, but when you're in high school you might start to look more like another body type. It all depends on your pre-determined genetic code and, in the final analysis, one body type is no better than another.

Eating disorders are conditions that can affect your mental and physical health. People who suffer from eating disorders become obsessed with losing or maintaining weight. They put most of their attention on the food (or lack of food) that they consume. Many young teens develop eating disorders because they feel that their bodies are inadequate and that they need to lose a drastic amount of weight.

If you ever feel that you are "too fat" or overweight and that it is not good to weigh too much, be careful because weighing too little is also bad for your health. If you think that you might have dietary or weight problems, you should visit a doctor rather than take matters into your own hands. Maintaining a healthy body comes through diet and exercise and a good balance of both. If you or a friend show signs of an eating disorder or a weight problem, tell an adult immediately and seek help because these problems can be extremely dangerous and detrimental to your health.

In summary, don't be obsessed about your body type; it will probably change. Also, maintain a healthy diet and exercise regularly. Parents, guardians and, if necessary, doctors can help with both eating disorders and weight problems.

Alexandra Clark
~11th grade

SURVIVAL SECRET:
Stay true to yourself.

CHAPTER 4
Moving in the Military

Growing up in a house with two older brothers, a dog and one parent may sound typical until you realize that your one and only parent is in the military. My life may seem very different in comparison to the average kid. Luckily, I believe that my life is pretty typical due to my mom's loving guidance and "chill" personality. Because my mom is in the military, I changed schools quite a bit. Having to attend three different middle schools in two different states before moving on to high school has taught me three major lessons about feeling comfortable and confident in a new school.

First, do not try to "re-invent the wheel." What I mean by that is don't try to make up a new personality just because you are somewhere new and want to "fit in." I learned that by staying true to myself I always found the real friends for whom I was looking. This viewpoint especially applies if you consider yourself strange or quirky. If you try to change yourself to fit the mold of a stereotypical cool kid you'll end up losing out on a chance to meet some truly cool kids who have very similar interests to yours.

I'll give an example of how this is true in my own life because it is how I first met one of my best friends. At the beginning of eighth grade, my school started a chess club at the library. I had just moved to a brand new school and thought that this would be a good place to meet people with similar hobbies. When I arrived at the library, I was handed a chessboard along with all the chess pieces. I sat down at an empty table and began to set up the board; then here came a kid at random. He asked me to play a match of chess. Of course, I replied: "Yes." As we began to play, we started talking about our lives. Then we realized that we were both brand new to the school. We also discovered that we enjoyed the same video games, played the same sports and even supported the same sports teams. Like that, we instantly became friends and we always had each other's backs. Even though he moved away, we still are best friends to this very day.

The second lesson I learned is to be aware of those who will try to take advantage of you because you are the new kid. This is a lesson that everyone will go through once in his or her life—for some, even more than once. This really applies to kids whom others consider "too nice," gullible or easily tricked. Once, a rather large boy saw me with a $20 bill and he tried to convince me that I should give it to him because he didn't have money in his lunch account. I offered to buy him lunch with money I had on my account. He replied "never mind." I wanted him to know that I would help him if he really needed help but that he could not take advantage of me. He never asked me again.

The third and last lesson that I learned was to make sure that I expressed myself. What I mean by this is that I made certain that I displayed my hidden gifts, talents and interests. Quite often, potential friends popped up out of nowhere. For this last advice, I won't share an experience with you. Instead, I want you to go ahead and express yourself. Display your gifts, talents and interests. Create your own experiences to share with the world!

Cameron Lucas
~10th grade

SURVIVAL SECRET:
Middle school is your opportunity
to learn how to learn.

CHAPTER 5
Grades Don't Matter

When I was in middle school, I remember asking my teachers over and over again why I needed to do well on whatever test or quiz we had that week and they would always give me the same answer: "Middle school is meant to prepare you for high school which is meant to prepare you for college." College seemed very far away when I was in sixth grade, but never the less I kept trying my hardest to get As in each subject and when I failed to do so, as I often did, I would be very upset, but I didn't really understand why. Here is the secret that I wish I had known when I was in middle school: your grades don't matter. That doesn't mean middle school students should just stop caring about school work: Far from it! What it means is that you have the freedom to make mistakes, a luxury that I wish I had as a junior in high school.

The reasons behind why middle school grades don't matter are quite simple, but the way they are put together is not. To understand them, we must look forward to high school. In high school, your grades matter a lot. The grades are compiled into a grade point average (GPA) which is basically your overall grade in high school. Your GPA helps colleges determine if they are going to admit you or if they are going to reject your application; but colleges don't look at your middle school grades. In short, middle school grades have little or no bearing on what is hopefully the ultimate goal of going to college.

However, if you are applying to private high schools or magnet schools, your grades will count. Highly selective independent schools and public schools that focus on high achievement in math and science will look at your transcript in order to be admitted.

Just because your grades may not matter in middle school doesn't mean you shouldn't work hard. Like my teacher said, middle school is meant to prepare you for high school and in high school your grades matter greatly. Middle school is your opportunity to learn how to learn. It's your opportunity to learn how best you take in information. You are free to experiment with different studying techniques to find out what works best for you. If one study technique doesn't work and you score badly on a test, there are no long term academic repercussions and you are free to try a different technique. The same goes for essays and other assignments.

When I was in middle school, I learned very quickly that I did not fully understand the books I was being assigned in English and, as a result, I was scoring badly on tests and quizzes. I soon discovered that I could better absorb the material if I used an audiobook. It is discoveries like this one that a student can make in middle school without a previous failure or impediment affecting any permanent record. As James Joyce said, "Mistakes are the portals of discovery." Don't be afraid to fail a little in middle school as long as you learn from it.

Middle school is also your opportunity to discover whom you are. You should use this time to draw if you like art or build things if you are interested in engineering. You have the freedom to discover what you like to do in middle school because your grades don't matter. Middle school can also be a big part of this discovery process. You can determine if you are good at science, music or sports and you can expand on that. In high school, there is little time to develop yourself in this way because there is always something else you can be doing to get into college and there is little time for personal fulfillment. This doesn't mean you should drop all school work and go to play football or video games, but it does mean that sometimes you can do so and you'll be fine.

Learning is not only very important to your future as a student, but it can also be very rewarding. Just because your grades in middle school have no bearing on your future careers doesn't mean you should ignore your education. Not only will a good middle school foundation help you when you go to high school, but it will also help you discover how you learn best. Use this time to learn from your failures and to correct them. Learning is one of the most enjoyable and important things you can experience in your life. Middle school is your chance to enjoy it without the stress of a GPA that matters. Make the most of it.

Christopher Wong
~11th grade

CHAPTER 6
Sports

One of the most difficult transitions that you will encounter in middle school involves the challenge of balancing academic studies and sports. As you transition to middle school, more is demanded of you from both your teachers and your coaches. They will want you to "be the best that you can be" in both sports and academic pursuits. You will notice that coaches in middle school who were content to observe you and your buddies playing in sand boxes in the lower grades, gradually start demanding more of the school athletes and want the students to take sports more seriously than they did previously. These coaches will start pushing you to meet your maximum skill levels and they expect that you will be willing to fight the urge to give up when you are in the training room and you are asked to do five more pushups or lift a few more weights.

You will also need to make sure that you receive sufficient sleep to ensure that you can balance all of the physical activities and studies. Making sure that you eat nutritious healthy meals should also help you maintain the stamina needed to keep up with the demands of both sports and studies.

The athletic programs are much more developed in middle school than in elementary school; therefore, you will find that middle school presents a great opportunity to try different sports (football, basketball, wrestling, lacrosse, golf, soccer, etc.) This should help you get a good sense as to which sports you would like to focus on in high school. Personally, I would recommend a sport that is growing more and more popular on the east coast: Lacrosse. The kids that start playing at an early age find that they have an advantage because they can play in tournaments throughout the region and become "known" in the sport.

In middle school, the administrators allow the athletes to leave classes early to travel to games with other schools. This is a huge responsibility and you must make sure that you coordinate with your teachers at least a day in advance so that you can get any assignments that you might miss from leaving early for "away" games. Also, letting your teacher know a day in advance helps to reinforce in his or her mind that you are a conscientious and serious student who cares about your studies. This will also provide the teacher with an opportunity to give you any handouts that you might miss while you are away. Finally, this will motivate the teacher to work with you to help you balance sports and studies.

Make sure that you keep the textbooks that you are not using at home as it may be harder for you to keep up and manage carrying your textbooks and sporting equipment on the bus to and from games. And you will want to be sure that you have a lock on your locker if you have expensive sports gear or equipment in it. Combination locks are the best. This will make your parents happy. They will not want to spend their evening at the sporting goods store purchasing equipment for you that has "gone missing." Share your combination with your coach and your parents in the event that one day you forget an essential textbook or a piece of equipment and you have to ask someone else to retrieve it for you.

I speak from experience. Now that I am in high school, I play on the school ice hockey team. My teammates and I are required to be at the skating rink for practice at 5 a.m. each morning. This requires tremendous coordination, organization and commitment to go to practice in the morning before school starts.

You will likely want to keep a schedule of the time that you wish to devote to sports and the time you will devote to studies. Above all else, you must make sure that you have reserved sufficient time for academic studies. You must take care of your education first and make that your priority. Sports should be the secondary concern. Your outlook during your middle school years should be that sports will always be there for you, but the opportunity to get the most out of your education which can lead to greater opportunities in the future may not be there. Great grades now can establish a pattern of high expectation and motivation which lend themselves to great grades in high school. Great grades in high school with a balance of sports can open many doors.

This holds true even if you are a sports fanatic and dream of one day going to the National Basketball Association (NBA), the National Football League (NFL) or another professional sports organization. It is a fact that one of the first items a potential recruiter looks at is a student's grades. The recruiter will ask for your transcript. In most cases where two students have equal talent and ability in their chosen sport, the recruiter will take the one with the better grades. There are also cases where one student is more talented than another in an athletic field but the recruiter selects the less talented athlete because of his higher grades.

High school counselors tell their students that the recruiter will actually select the child with the better grades because he knows that there is no question that he can ultimately get that student admitted to the college where the student's academic profile (cumulative GPA and SAT scores, etc.) meets the criteria of the school's admissions office. College admission standards are very competitive these days. Some of the top schools only admit 15 per cent of the applicants. When the college recruiter knows that he can easily "sell" a student to the admissions committee because that student easily meets the committee's admission criteria, that recruiter may be inclined to expend his valuable time, energy and effort trying to recruit the student who is a sure thing rather than spend his time with a borderline student whom the admissions committee might ultimately reject.

There may be days when you find that you have to miss practice in order to complete your studies (e.g. a research paper or an exam). It may be painful, but don't worry, maintaining an "academics first" attitude and outlook will pay off in the long run. This academics first approach will ensure that you will not fall behind in your extremely important core subjects (math, science, English). As an added bonus, an academics first attitude during the week will ensure that you do not have to do catch up studies over the weekend. As someone who has "been there; done that," please be sure to enjoy your care free days in middle school because high school and college are increasingly demanding!

That is the extent of my advice. If you follow these rules you should be in good shape.

Jeffery Lewis
~10th Grade

SURVIVAL SECRET:
If you are having trouble in class, tell someone.

CHAPTER 7
Teachers

Dealing with teachers can be very hard in middle school. There is more work to complete and more after school activities in which to participate. In addition, you are expected to be more independent and to receive less help from your parents. You may feel that your teachers are annoying or frustrating you; but there are ways to make your experiences easier. Here are a few things to help you deal with middle school teachers:

1. Always be respectful and polite. School is a place to learn and teachers spend many hours planning to help you learn. You should not look at your cellphone or other electronic devices, talk to your friends or do homework for other classes while you are supposed to be paying

attention to the teacher. Some kids may think that it is "no big deal," but teachers really enjoy seeing students learn. Showing interest could motivate the teachers to make the lessons more interesting. Some students may talk back and disrupt classes but you should not do that because it is rude and unruly and it might hurt the teacher's feelings.

2. Try to get to know your teachers. Many teachers have a routine as to when assignments are due and what assignments they give. That way you can make a routine for yourself and figure out when you can study and fit in your assignments with other activities.

3. If you are having trouble in your class, tell someone. All classes are places to learn and you are not supposed to know all of the information from the very beginning. Many teachers have after school time that they set aside for students to come in and get help. This is also helpful because it provides extra time to get to know your teacher and your teacher gets to know you. Getting to know your teacher helps your teacher to understand you and how you learn. Your parents can also assist you in getting extra help.

4. Do your assignments on time so that you don't fall behind and must ask the teacher at the last minute to help you. Teachers try to be clear about what assignments are due and when they are due. If you are ever not certain about an assignment, make sure to ask about it as soon as

possible. Otherwise, teachers may feel that you are taking advantage of a situation if you continually fall behind and then you expect them to help you catch up.

Teachers in middle school understand their students and enjoy working with them. This may not be always clear to the students. The teachers want to see you trying to learn and then they are more willing to help you. The most important thing is to try to talk to people about your problems. Talking with your teacher, parent or other authority figure is the best way to make sure both you and your teachers have a positive experience.

Anthony Eaton, Jr.
~7th grade

SURVIVAL SECRET:
Perseverance is necessary for survival.

CHAPTER 8
Bullying

Adversity is defined as "a condition marked by unhappiness, misfortune, or distress." But hard times can create resilience and resourcefulness. As a middle schooler in the sixth grade, I was ostracized for being different. Because my peers bullied me for my differences, I learned to deal with difficulties and to develop leadership skills.

My transition from elementary to middle school was not pleasant because of race, class and intellectual and physical differences. Back then, I was taller than most kids my age and I was overweight with glasses, a retainer, acne and an extremely high pitched voice. I was brutally chastised by my peers for these dissimilarities.

As an only child, I was always better able to relate to adults than to my peers. At the time, my intellect surpassed the average person of eleven years of age; but my intellectual growth was unaccompanied by the social maturity that was needed to supplement such knowledge. I tried and failed to relate properly to my peers. I tried to act and dress like others; however, it was not my true self. Soon I spiraled into self-doubt and despair.

I was not happy with life and I completely withdrew socially. At lunch every day, I sat alone; I sulked over my lack of social acceptance. Inclusion and acceptance were all I desired. Friends from elementary school became distant. I did not fit into a particular social circle. I was neither "black enough" to be accepted by my black peers, nor was I "white enough" to be accepted into the tight knit white social circle. I was rejected by my own gender as I did not play sports nor was I disrespectful to girls. I felt alone. On the weekends, while my schoolmates got together at the mall or went to the movies, I stayed in my room contemplating my lack of a social life.

At the time, it was common to text constantly with friends. However, my cellphone was a barren wasteland with sent messages but never a response. My thoughts were clouded by the slurs that I endured every day. When I walked into the classroom, I instantly became the topic of discussion. People talked about my skin color, my mannerism, my clothes and my speech as if it were assumed that my sole existence was to answer the inappropriate questions of others. One of the most painful experiences occurred when I was called the "N word" in front of the whole class. Constant verbal abuse weighed heavily on the soul.

I wanted to leave my middle school and quietly transfer to a private school. However, my parents did not allow me to do so. My parents knew that if I left my middle school that I would not learn how to confront adversity. They felt that I would learn that running away from problems was the only way to deal with obstacles. My mom would say: "If you leave, you will take yourself with you."

This forced me to combat the evils that I faced on a daily basis. I had no other choice but to grow up and learn how to deal with hardship. I learned that I could not change other people, but I could only change myself. I stopped engaging the bullies. I no longer had cutting responses for their taunts. I ignored their ignorance.

I stopped trying to be a part of the crowd and I was unafraid to be by myself. This has been a large contributing factor to my boldness. I am unafraid to challenge either my peers, authority or the status quo. I was able to gain a unique view of life and the world. I was able to find my true self.

As difficult experiences can elicit hidden skills, I began to assert my social independence. With time, I became more emotionally intelligent and compassionate. These traits allowed me to help others with their personal struggles. I was able to abandon the desire for popularity and I was able to create meaningful and lasting friendships.

Another trait that being bullied elicited was my transition from a follower to a leader. I was able to think freely without the pressure of peers. As I realized my leadership potential, I found the ability to influence others positively, the facility to build consensus and the ability to lead others to desired outcomes. This allows me to manage others and projects when working in collective efforts. Without such negative experiences in middle school, I would have continued to isolate myself from the world.

The Roman poet, Horace, stated: "Adversity has the effect of eliciting talents which in prosperous circumstances would have lain dormant." Bullying revealed my leadership skills and nurtured emotional resilience. Perseverance is difficult; however, it was necessary for my survival.

Middle school does not last forever. It does get better. Recently, I was asked by an acquaintance from middle school: "How are you able to be so nice to all the people who have wronged you, including me?" I replied, "I can't live my life being angry at everyone."

Ross Cooper
~11th grade

SURVIVAL SECRET:
Serious relationships can take focus away from studies.

CHAPTER 9
Dating

Dating is a popular topic in middle school. Kids in 6th, 7th and 8th grades stop having "play dates" and begin having get-togethers with groups that include girls and boys. Also, this is the time when schools have dances where you can bring a date. At this stage, many girls and boys want to meet someone who will be a boyfriend or girlfriend. Kids start becoming less shy around people of the opposite gender and may like each other as more than just friends. This awakening is normal and will continue throughout life. While this attraction is a natural occurrence, there are positives and negatives to seeing someone at a young age.

During this time, relationships typically are not serious but can be an introduction into the world of real dating. Middle school dating lets you learn about people in a different way and it also gives you an idea of what you like and dislike about people. It is a positive thing because it prepares you for future serious relationships.

For some students, middle school can be a difficult time and dating may further complicate a student's life. While many kids are dealing with massive changes in their lives, a relationship that is filled with drama will only make matters worse. At this time, most parents stress the importance of school and preparing for high school. Trying to have a serious relationship can take your focus away from studies and other activities. It is not uncommon for parents to put an end to dating if the relationship becomes too much of an interference.

Aside from the distractions, dating can affect other friendships. When you are seeing someone, childhood friends who have been the focus of your attention for many years often feel left out and resentful. These negative feelings may result in tension and can end friendships. If your childhood friends and your boyfriend or girlfriend attend the same school, maintaining friendships can be very complicated.

These are the advantages and disadvantages of dating in middle school. It can be both exciting and challenging. Dating allows you to understand the differences in people. More importantly, dating can help you to understand yourself.

Jay Pendarvis, Jr.
~7th grade

SURVIVAL SECRET:
Don't abandon your identity to fit in.

CHAPTER 10
The Only One

I will be discussing the topic of *being one of the only, perhaps the only, African American* student at middle school. I will be sharing my stories and perspectives on things that I had to go through as a middle school student. And I will share how it has made me a stronger person today.

Now, as a sophomore in high school, I can reflect over my middle school days and think about how hard, yet empowering, my experiences were. I now attend a school that is 50 percent African American. My current school has been a huge adjustment for me but it has allowed me to interact with people that look like me.

During my middle school days, I went through a lot of changes. I transferred from the school that I had been attending for five years to a small school where I knew no one. My middle school was smaller than you would expect. It was so small in relation to the number of students in other schools that I was the only African American girl in the entire middle school.

At first, it was kind of a shock to be the only African American girl, but I realized that it wouldn't really be much of a change. At my previous school I was one of only seven African American girls out of 80 students. So I guess you could say that my experiences were not the most racially diverse. All of my life, I had been attending schools which were predominantly white. All my friends were white and there wasn't any real problem with it. I was comfortable with the friends that I had and they didn't care about me being African American.

Some days I felt I didn't fit in. My friends always were talking about things that I didn't necessarily understand or of which I had no knowledge. My friends never treated me differently but they would talk about people that looked like me in a negative way. Using myself as an example, I would try to give my input about the stereotype and say that these statements or comments do not apply to all African Americans. Their response was always something like: "But Gabby you're not really black." Really black! What does that even mean? Does it mean that I don't fit the average stereotype of an African American girl? I guess you could say that; but never the less the negative comments still hurt.

As we all got older, we started having stronger opinions on different things such as politics, education, community service and race. Although we agreed on most things, there was always one thing that we disagreed on and that was race. My friends were always talking about how black people are so loud and rude. And again I felt trapped. I felt as though I had to defend something that was much bigger than just myself. I would try with all my might to either give a very informative and factual point of view or try to move to a different topic. I continued to stand up for my race through middle school and in my freshman year in high school.

From a girl's perspective, I think one of the most difficult things that African American children have to go through while being at a predominately white school is that when you like a boy that doesn't look like you, you are always faced with the possibility of him not liking you because of your skin color. Sometimes it may not even be the boy, it may be his parents who say: "Yeah, sure, she is a good friend but not a good girlfriend." Such rejection can be painful. This experience has made me stronger.

Being the only African American person at school can also put you in the strange position of people asking questions about your hair. In middle school after physical education classes it was a daily activity to see how my hair stayed in its upright position. My friends would touch and play with my hair. They always asked: "How does your hair do that?" My response was always the same: "I have to keep my hair moisturized." At first it was funny; but afterwards, it escalated to a point where I was annoyed. I felt that I was being treated as if I were in a museum. Always being looked at and asked a million questions to which I didn't even know the answers sometimes. But, again, these experiences and the constant bombardment with questions gave me a different perspective on life that has helped to bolster my self-esteem.

Gabrielle Stevenson
~10th grade

SURVIVAL SECRET:
Fear is not the answer.

CHAPTER 11
Gym

Throughout middle school, gym always seems to be the most hated class among students. Although gym is regarded as a sweaty tiring interruption to a day of academic studies, there are some hidden benefits. These benefits will reveal themselves if you approach this class in the right manner and without fear.

Changing clothes for gym is an uncomfortable experience for many students of both genders. Changing in front of your peers shouldn't embarrass you. Your body is unique, and you shouldn't stress over the opinions of your peers. Your time in the locker room isn't the appropriate time to stress out over the various features on your body; it's simply to change from your school clothes into your gym uniform and vice versa. Changing your clothes should only take you a few minutes at most. If changing with other people around stresses you, then try changing in the bathroom stall, shower stall, or possibly the nurse's office.

The inescapable fact about gym is that it involves physical exercise. Don't be fearful. Exercise leads to sweat, body odor and the occasional physical pain. Deodorant is a must-have, and a regular sized stick will last you through most of the school year. Try to refrain from using excessive amounts of perfume or cologne after gym because sweet scents and sweat don't mix very well. If you sweat more than average, or if you enjoy an extra-fresh feeling, keep bath wipes and a small towel in your gym locker. Try to keep extra socks with your gym uniform. The smell emanating from dirty socks and from sweaty feet may be torturous for you and everyone around you. Most of all, remember to wash your gym uniform. Periodically popping your uniform in the washing machine will prevent your teenage body odor from radiating throughout the gym. Buying multiple uniforms can also save some time from having to maintain the same uniform throughout the year.

Sometimes, many students aren't motivated to participate in gym. The goal and focus of the course is to provide students with physical exercise and to teach them about healthy habits. Participation is the backbone of the course. If you're concerned about your level of physical fitness and you are afraid of embarrassing yourself in front of your classmates, remember that everyone has a different level of physical fitness; you don't have to fit into a particular mold. Some of the students in your class might play sports, so they'll naturally be at a higher level of physical fitness than those who don't. Trying your best and working hard will get you through gym class just like every other class you take.

Generally, injuries are an inevitable part of life. I have personally suffered from multiple ankle sprains and a concussion. A note from a doctor or parent is usually required in order to be excused from gym participation. Some teachers will ask that alternative assignments that pertain to health and wellness be completed. If your injury is serious, you shouldn't play around with the other students in gym even if you think that you are being careful. An accident could lead to longer recovery time or to more injuries. If you think you might have injured yourself during class, then you should tell your teacher immediately so that you can go to the school nurse and address the injury.

Initially, gym seems to be an annoying and useless class, but exercising for as little as 15 minutes a day helps to prevent future problems in your body. As long as you try your best, you'll find that gym isn't as worthless as its reputation paints it to be. Overall, gym can be extremely beneficial if you keep a positive attitude. Don't be too concerned about the overall gym experiences.

Alexandra Clark
~11th grade

SURVIVAL SECRET:
Check your planner daily.

CHAPTER 12
Organization

Imagine yourself rushing into middle school, hurrying to get to 1st period. You're already late and arrive in class only to find out that you don't have your homework. As a matter of fact, you didn't even know that you had homework. Now you have a lunch detention and you have to do your homework with your teacher while your friends are at lunch enjoying themselves.

Using an organizational tool such as a planner for this particular situation probably would have prevented this whole mess from even occurring in its entirety. By using organizational tools, problems and related issues could be avoided and valuable skills could be developed. Development of these skills could greatly impact you today in middle school and in the future.

There are many tools that are available to you in school. Some may benefit you, but others may not. You'll have to explore your options and see which one is the best. You could use the planner, already mentioned, to keep up with homework and other projects for all your classes. By using a planner it almost guarantees that you won't forget anything as long as you write in it. With this particular one all it takes is for you to check your planner every day to make sure that you don't fall behind and, as a result, are unsuccessful in school.

Sectioning off your binders will also be quite helpful for your classes. This tool keeps you from losing worksheets and homework. Sectioning is also very useful whether your teacher says you need it or not. It also saves time when trying to get work done by allowing you to flip to any section easily. Using visual techniques such as colors and patterns also makes keeping up with things easier. By using these techniques it makes grabbing binders in a hurry much faster and easier by just looking at them. All these tools may be helpful to you right now but they could also be really helpful throughout your whole life.

The tools previously listed can help you become a very hard working, organized student that could help shape your career. Tackling huge workloads of homework at school could also be easier to handle.

These tools prepare you to tackle these workloads with ease and sufficiency.

Success in school is proven to come from organization and time management. In general, developing these skills will help you in school by getting things done quickly and getting great grades. Organizational tools affect time management extremely throughout your academic career.

Getting things done quickly allows you to have more free time to play sports and hang out with friends. These tools are not just effective in school though, they are also effective outside of school; they come in handy on and off the job.

The tools listed also help train your mind to use certain skills that come in handy throughout your daily life. In some experiences a lot of these tools are commonly used outside of school to make simple or critical decisions. In career and work experiences, depending on what you do, use of these skills and techniques could vary from organizing paperwork to keeping track of all the employees of a huge company.

These tools are even great for planning out your best path in life, for example, they help you decipher which career path is best for you based on your best interest. In conclusion, these tools can be used not only in school but also outside of school and you can use them throughout all your life experiences.

Brianna Latham
~8th grade

SURVIVAL SECRET:
Bring your own lunch if the cafeteria serves "mystery meat."

CHAPTER 13
Private to Public Charter School

I like having friends at school, but you can go from being a social butterfly to being an outcast when you change schools. Transitioning from private school to an urban public charter school was difficult, in part, because the basic transition to a different school and its environments is difficult. The private school experience and the urban public charter school experience are very different. There is a slight distinction to be made between urban public schools and urban public charter schools.

Currently, I attend an urban public charter school. In urban public charter schools, students are required to wear uniforms. When I started at the urban public charter school, I thought it was an urban public school. Prior to this point, I went to private school. Parents must apply for their children to be interviewed and tested before admission to urban public charter schools; this is similar to the private school acceptance process. I didn't know the difference between public and urban public charter schools. Although students at an urban public charter school wear uniforms, they wear whatever they want to wear with the uniform and have no compunction about dressing freely.

For me, one of the main differences between private school and my urban public charter school was that I was virtually friendless when I changed schools. Since I skipped two grades when I transferred, I was much younger than my peers. I had started school when I was two years old, so there was actually a three year gap in age between my classmates and me. The age difference made it even more difficult for me to "blend in," to act natural and to make friends.

The next biggest issue about transferring to an urban public charter school was the lunch. At the private school, the cafeteria had both hot and cold bars where you could make a salad of any kind or opt for a turkey sandwich on toast points. When I transferred, I learned about a thing called "mystery meat." There's a reason why they call it "mystery meat." I'm almost certain that my current school lunches are not made of real food. They are made of square, indistinguishable, tasteless muck. I did a research project on "mystery meat" when I was in

6th grade and you won't be surprised to know that I didn't find anything. This was one of the first ways by which I was traumatized in middle school. I solved that problem by bringing my own lunch. I think you should too.

There were other things that were new to me once I transferred from private school. Every day I had to walk past a security guard and through a metal detector. That was not the case in private school. Also, when I started fifth grade, my homeroom teacher did an "ice breaker" on the first day of school. "That's normal, right?" I was shocked that one of the questions asked was how many books we had in our homes. I didn't answer that question for two reasons: there were too many books to count and the question itself didn't make sense to me. My teacher (as well as all the other teachers in the school) assumed that it was her responsibility to introduce the students and their parents to the idea of college. For my urban public charter school teachers, it was an assumption that students needed to be told that they could go to college after high school. As for my private school teachers and parents, college was a natural expectation after high school.

Teachers were a big change for me in transitioning because I went from having an experienced middle-aged lady and her teaching assistant to someone who was a year and a half out of college and who, essentially, was learning along with us. I remember that in 7th grade, my English teacher gave our class a book he had just read in college two years prior. He was basically trying to give it to us while it was fresh in his mind. This was absurd because he was throwing very harsh, mature issues at 13 year olds, and of course, at me - the one 11 year-old in the grade.

Interactions with teachers and peers improved tremendously when I started high school. By that time, my age was not so much of a factor and I had been with the same group of students since sixth grade. High school is not like all the clichés in the movies where the little guy is constantly picked on and no one comes to his rescue. Based on my observations in my school, there isn't anyone who is picked on individually or consistently. There isn't a "jock squad" that goes around and beats up the nerds or dunks their heads in the toilets. We don't sing "Kumbaya," but we do stick up for each other occasionally.

My experience in an urban public charter high school has not been all bad. There are positives, more positives than negatives. That's what makes it different from the movies. Unfortunately, middle school is just like the movies. I am sad to say that I actually have seen someone stuffed into his locker.

Most often, for private school kids, being privileged is taken for granted. No matter how normal being a public school kid is for some of you guys, to a private school student the public school might as well be a foreign country. Having gone to an urban public charter school for so long, I'm pretty much used to it now; but it's still a bit uncomfortable from time to time when I don't understand some of the most recent urban slangs.

I have never been one to gawk at pretty things. When I started at the urban public charter school, I saw that some of my peers were impressed with some of the material things with which I was accustomed. Even through all of this, the most important thing to know about transferring is that there are always the same personalities. You will always have the class clown, although he may be kept in check more in a private school setting. There will be the anorexics and the bulimics. You will always have the mean girl squad, the druggies, the nerds, the bookworms, the kids who think they are cool but will always submit to the real popular kids and finally the outliers: the children who don't really belong anywhere, know it, and don't make any noticeable effort to change it.

I was a bookworm for the first couple of years. I stayed with my books because no one could really bear to be around me for reasons that my naïve mind couldn't grasp. There was an abundance of jealousy at my being significantly younger and on their intellectual level. My thought process was that I was only smart enough to do the same work as kids who were older than I and it was no big deal, but later I realized that I was just that young and just that innocent. I was too young to know.

I didn't realize how frustrating, even infuriating, it was to be a ten or eleven year old student in fifth grade with a girl who had just turned eight and she was capable of doing the same work as you. That made my classmates angry and it got me bullied. I hated being in school because it just meant eight hours of loneliness, sadness and stress; but I wasn't ever exactly alone. There was always someone to make fun of me for something, usually something that didn't make sense; but the reason it hurt was because that person had gone to the effort to make me feel bad. Thinking back on the power of those daily insults that hit like grenades, I realize now how petty kids can be and that today the same hurtful efforts would have about the same impact as being pelted with cotton balls. I'm stronger now and perhaps always was but probably never had a need to use it until changing school environments. I felt awful because I didn't know how to ignore them and it hurt me. It hurt me all the time.

Adults often comment when a child has a particularly radiant smile or personality. I've always been a fairly quiet person and as a child I was almost always cooperative. Being bullied didn't make me submissive in any way; but it did make me quieter for a time. After that I was much louder, more boisterous and always spoke my mind. I realized that I had been letting people walk all over me and that they were using me to make themselves feel better, and I finally put a stop to it. As a high school junior I still speak my mind and I no longer let my negative classmates have their emotional way with me. To quote Invictus by Williams Ernest Henley, "I am the master of my fate. I am the captain of my soul."

Jelani Brooks
~11th grade

Jelani Brooks
~11th grade

SURVIVAL SECRET:
The most helpful advice comes from people who already attend the school.

CHAPTER 14
Transitions

The transition from elementary school to middle school can be exciting, challenging, or even frightening. Each person's experience is unique; therefore, there is no way to be absolutely prepared for all the encounters to come. However, from a young woman's perspective, there are many social, emotional and physical changes that are expected to occur during this time.

One common concern is making new friends. Middle school, in essence, is a completely foreign environment and the new setting may be intimidating. People tend to behave much differently than they would in elementary school; this can mostly be accredited to the age difference. The ability to adjust to the setting is key. The most efficient way to do so is to be you. Just think, each and every incoming middle school student is in the exact same position as you. It is inevitable that you will find a group of people that have common interests with you. So, just relax and take a deep breath because the nervous feelings are undoubtedly mutual and will soon subside.

Another issue that you will encounter is the process of going through puberty. As you become a young adult, not only will you grow socially but you will also mature physically. Young women grow breasts, become curvier, and have their first period, while young men grow taller and acquire broader shoulders and deeper voices. Although the changes may seem somewhat sudden, they are undeniably normal. The most important things to remember are to keep up with personal hygiene, maintain a healthy diet and appreciate all of the phases of your constantly changing appearance.

Also, during middle school, troubling emotions often arise. Your thoughts may be overlooked by some of your peers. They may see sharing emotions as uncool or a sign of weakness. In truth, it is imperative to pay attention to what goes on in your mind. Most importantly, do not keep what is inside. Oftentimes, sharing your feelings with others (whether those feelings are positive or negative) can instill a sense of security in such an ever-changing time period. Other outlets include keeping a journal, engaging in athletic activities or turning feelings into an art form.

The most intimidating attribute of all may be the school itself. You may often hear rumors about getting lost in the wrong part of the school or about nasty, rotten lunches. However, the rumors are almost always exaggerated. Additionally, the school will most likely hold orientations so that you can familiarize yourself with the building. For more reassurance, try to muster up the courage to ask an older student. The most helpful advice comes from people that already attend the school.

In conclusion, a major component of middle school is change. It is a time when you are forced to step out of your comfort zone as social, physical and emotional changes make their way into your life. Although nerve-racking, middle school is something to look forward to. Most often, the terrifying rumors are untrue. Ultimately, to survive middle school, it is critical to love the skin you're in and enjoy what the exciting future holds.

Aria Townes
~9th grade

SURVIVAL SECRET:
Do not confuse self-expression
with sensationalism.

CHAPTER 15
Trust

In adolescence, you will begin to assert your independence. You will branch out from your family and begin to confide in other people who may not be relatives. Learning whom to trust is a big issue in middle school. When confidences are broken, it can lead to conflict. However, you can learn to navigate situations that can stem from the betrayal of trust.

During middle school, you will begin to express your individuality. Self-expression should not be confused with sensationalism. There may be a tendency to "hype" or exaggerate accomplishments or actions. Your peers or you may "tell it all" for social gain. In telling one's own business or the information of others, there is sometimes a feeling of power associated with imparting news. However, this empowerment may be fleeting. "So-called" friends are liable to tell any and everything, from the mundane to the scandalous. By telling your own business or spreading gossip about others, you can devalue and discredit your social standing and lose valuable friends.

It is never good to be labeled an "attention seeker." If the nature of what is breached is outrageous, gossip may spread throughout the school and possibly to administration or guidance professionals. Depending on the circumstances of the breached information, teachers and counselors at school have a professional obligation to resolve the conflict. This can be done in a variety of ways: peer mediation, parental intervention, or in the worst case scenario, the police.

Of course, you should not involve yourself with gossip. You should take care as social media can be sources of hearsay and rumor. Nevertheless, when trust has been breached, it is important to address the situation. You can avoid creating further conflict by not letting the issue fester. If the situation is not addressed, the gossipers may feel validated and that they have accomplished something by sharing someone's secret.

It is necessary to make the gossiper aware of what he or she has done, why it was wrong and how he or she should go about reconciling the situation as soon as possible. If you wait to do so, the situation could implode and could have drastic effects on you and on your peer group. In the short term, to advocate for your friends or yourself may be difficult; however, it will set a precedent for future dealings. You will learn not to be afraid of those who have betrayed your trust.

There is a lot of peer pressure to reveal what you know. My advice to you is to be careful about whom you trust, what you share about yourself and what you say to others. Do not spread scandal or negativity. Always try to be positive, respectful and kind. In this way, you will preserve your information, reputation and self-respect.

Ross Cooper

~11th grade

SURVIVAL SECRET:
Don't pay attention to drama.

CHAPTER 16
A Family's Experiences

Our family includes 3 siblings: Brandon, Kayla and Lauren. Middle school was a big step for us after leaving elementary school. In elementary school, there was basically one teacher who taught mostly all of our courses except art and music. Since, we were in one room most of the day with the same classmates, there were no worries about being late to class for a particular course. We kept all our books in our desks. There was not a lot of gossip or drama since the same students were together all day in a small classroom setting.

However, middle school was totally different. There were many more people in the school. There were lots of gossip and rumors about people. So, don't associate with these types of people because it will eventually cause problems. Stay out of trouble. Don't pay attention to drama. Lauren indicated that girls have problems staying out of drama.

This implies that you should choose your friends wisely. Be friends with people who don't start or participate in drama or gossip. Also, due to the fact that we realized that peer pressure started at middle school, we suggest that you don't let your friends get you in trouble. Don't do anything that makes you feel uncomfortable or that you think is wrong whether it is to yourself or to someone else.

Brandon pointed out that one of the most difficult challenges for him was to learn how to balance responsibilities with fun. Brandon enjoyed playing sports to the point that he neglected resting or completing assignments on time. Brandon recommends that learning how to study and complete class assignments while having fun should be mastered in middle school. If this is possible, it will make high school a lot easier when your grades really count.

Brandon and Lauren thought having a locker would be more challenging than it was. Learn how to work your combination locker. If you can attend the "open house" prior to school starting, practice your combination locker until you have mastered it. Then it becomes a piece of cake.

Kayla was amazed about changing classes throughout the day. Due to the fact that a student changes classes for the different courses during middle school, we also recommend that you attend open house so you can learn where each class is located. Don't do a lot of chatting in the hallways between classes, because this will cause you to be late for class. The teacher will then give you a tardy and it remains on your record. Not good.

Follow these recommendations for middle school, and you will survive. We did.

Brandon Joyner
~12th grade
Lauren Joyner
~9th grade
Kayla Joyner
~9th grade

SURVIVAL SECRET:
Use your time wisely.

CHAPTER 17
Balance

Find balance between school and other activities. School is one of the most important parts of your teen years. Middle school prepares you to handle great academic challenges, social challenges and, most of all, high school. Many students participate in various activities outside of class: including sports, performing arts and leadership groups. Finding a balance between these activities and school is important in order to maintain good grades while getting to all of your activities. Using your spare time wisely is important if you don't want to stay up all night doing homework. If you find yourself with some spare time, get some homework done. No matter how much time you may have, you'll at least be able to accomplish a portion of your homework. After all, slow and steady wins the race.

If you're not susceptible to motion sickness, then utilizing time in the car or on the bus will get your homework done faster than if you wait until you get home. Procrastination is your worst enemy when it comes to getting your homework done. It's important to start on your homework as soon as you can, because if you wait too long, you may find yourself scrambling to finish in the morning or during another class.

School comes first, so before watching TV or scrolling through twitter, you should work on your school assignments. Keeping your schoolwork organized will also ensure that you will be able to find all of the materials that you need to do your homework and study. If you accidentally miss one homework assignment, it's not the end of the world. However, you shouldn't make a habit of not doing your homework. Missing assignments add up, and they slowly drag your grades down. If you participate in many different activities, then you will most likely find yourself running back and forth between these activities and with very little free time in the middle.

It is important to eat all of your meals, and to have a couple of snacks throughout the day to keep your energy up. The time will come when you have to choose between two activities. You'll have to explain to your teacher, coach or another authority figure why you can't make it to a practice, rehearsal, or meeting. These decisions can be hard, but while making them, consider which is more important. Sometimes a deal can be worked out with your coaches so that you won't be punished for choosing one activity over another. If you feel extremely overwhelmed, then you might be participating in too many activities. It's okay to cut back on the number of activities in which you participate.

Remember to thank your parents or guardians for everything that they do for you. They most likely pay for the activities in which you are involved. Also, they drive you to and from the various events and functions. They sacrifice much of their personal time to ensure that you have all that you need.

Alexandra Clark
~11th grade

ABOUT THE AUTHORS

Ross Cooper is a high school junior. He is a member of the National Honor Society, the French Honor Society, the "It's Academic Team" and the Garden Club. He is the Teen Foundation Chair of his Jack and Jill Chapter. His hobbies include photography and music. He enjoys studying world history and the African diaspora. Ross is a proud vegan.

Jelani Brooks is a 15 year old high school junior. She is the Recording Secretary of her Jack and Jill Chapter. She is a member of her school's honors choir. She is also a member of the softball team and poetry club. Her hobbies include illustrations of Mandala art of Buddhist and Hindu spheres, music, poetry and reading.

Alexandra Clark is a high school junior. She participates in Symphonic Band, Color Guard, and Dance. She previously served as Teen Protocol Chair for the Eastern Region of Jack and Jill of America, Inc. and currently serves as Regional Teen Secretary.

Anthony Eaton, Jr. is a 7th grade honor roll student. He plays football and basketball and runs track. He enjoys attending church and playing video games.

Brandon Joyner is a high school senior. His hobbies include playing sports, especially basketball. He is currently the Teen Parliamentarian of his Jack and Jill Chapter. He is a proud Eagle Scout and plans to attend college in the fall.

Kayla Joyner is a high school freshman. Her hobbies include playing basketball and softball. She is active in girl scouts and is currently a senior scout. She enjoys having a twin sister.

Lauren Joyner is a high school freshman. Her hobbies include playing volleyball and basketball. She is active in girl scouts and is currently a senior scout. She enjoys having a twin sister.

Brianna Latham is an 8th grade honors student. She is involved in Symphonic Band and Future Business Leaders of America. She enjoys basketball, tennis and volleyball. She is active in her church and participates in the Youth Orchestra and Girl Scouts. Brianna is passionate about entertainment and technology. She serves as Teen Treasurer in her Jack and Jill Chapter.

Jeffrey Lewis is a high school sophomore. He plays on his high school varsity football team. He also plays on his high school junior varsity lacrosse and ice hockey teams. His hobbies include sports and music. He enjoys studying mathematics and business related topics.

Cameron Lucas is a high school sophomore. A self-proclaimed "military brat," Cameron is a member of DECA. He is on the varsity football team and his hobbies include winning video games, playing basketball and spending time with friends.

Jay Pendarvis, Jr. is a 13 year old 7th grader. He is an honors student and a member of the Drama club. He has a great love for music and enjoys playing the guitar. He is also a member of the track team and has won numerous awards in track and field.

Gabrielle Stevenson is a high school sophomore. She is a member of the high school swim team, the Onyx Club, Diamonds Club and her school's Gospel performing choir. She is the owner of her own business, "Under the Sea," where she instructs students on water safety and swimming techniques. She has also started a foundation "Gabby's Help Homeless." At church, she serves as the Worship Leader and sings in the choir. She is the current Teen Vice-President in her Jack and Jill Chapter.

Aria Townes is a high school freshman. She is pursuing an honors curriculum. She is a member of the POMS Dance Team and swims competitively. She is an active member of her church where she participates in the Senior Youth Ministry, Gospel Inspirers Choir and Girl Scouts. Her hobbies include baking, spending time with friends and swimming.

Malachi Walker is a high school senior and the Teen President of his Jack and Jill Chapter. He is an Eagle Scout and is on the varsity golf team and the Scholastic Bowl Team. His hobbies include video games, basketball and football.

Christopher Wong is a high school junior. He is a member of the National Honor Society, Model United Nations, TRYKA Film Coalition and is an active member of Student Government. He enjoys studying domestic politics, filmmaking, and international relations.

Jack and Jill of America, Inc.
Alexandria-Mount Vernon Chapter
Teen Foundation Committee
2014-2015

Committee Chairman
Ross Cooper
Committee Members
Jelani Brooks
Alexandra Clark
Brianna Latham
Jay Pendarvis, Jr.

Jack and Jill of America, Inc.

Established in 1938, Jack and Jill of America, Inc. is a social welfare organization with headquarters in Washington, D.C. With over 230 chapters, 10,000 mothers and 30,000 family members across the United States, the group dedicates its resources to improving the quality of life of children.

Jack and Jill of America Foundation, Inc.

Jack and Jill of America Foundation, Inc. is the philanthropic arm of Jack and Jill of America, Inc. Since its inception in 1968, the Foundation has distributed millions of dollars to communities all across America. The Foundation supports programs that not only create opportunities and challenges for children to learn and practice leadership skills, but also to build leadership character in youth.

The Alexandria-Mount Vernon Chapter

Officially chartered in 1966, the Alexandria-Mount Vernon (Virginia) Chapter is committed to the collective cultural, social and educational development of children as well as service to the City of Alexandria, Fairfax County and the surrounding communities.

SURVIVAL SECRETS OF MIDDLE SCHOOL

Made in the USA
Middletown, DE
15 February 2019